MAPWORLDS
WATER

©1996 Franklin Watts

First American Edition 1996 by
Franklin Watts
A Division of Grolier Publishing
Sherman Turnpike
Danbury, CT 06816

Library of Congress Cataloging in Publication Data

Parham, Molly
    Water / Molly Perham and Julian Rowe.
        p.cm.–(MapWorlds)
    Includes index.
    ISBN 0-531-14361-9
    1. Water—Juvenile literature. (1 Water) I. Rowe, Julian
II. Title. III. Series.
    GB662.3.P47 1995   94-39691
    553.7—dc20   CIP AC

Editorial planning: Serpentine Editorial
Design and typesetting: R & B Creative Services Ltd
Color origination: R & B Creative Services Ltd
Illustrations: Sallie Alane Reason

Photographic credits:
Chris Fairclough Colour Library cover (right), 10, 11, 15, 16, 17, 21, 26,
29 (below); Robert Harding Picture Library cover (top and below), title page;
The Hutchison Library 13 (top and below), 19, 27; Daniel Lodge 24; Julian
Rowe 14; Trip Cover (left), 9 (top and below), 18, 20, 23, 25, 30, Zefa 6-
7, 23, 29 (top).

10 9 8 7 6 5 4 3 2 1
Printed in Great Britain

MAPWORLDS
WATER

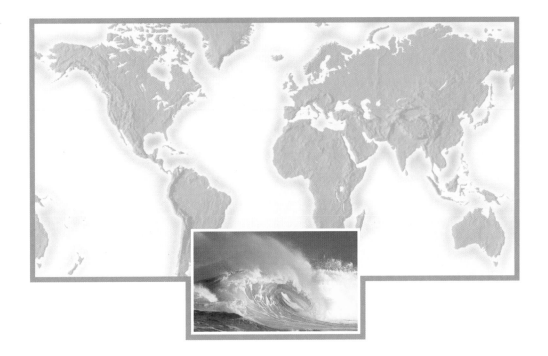

Molly Perham
and Julian Rowe

Illustrated by Sallie Alane Reason

FRANKLIN WATTS
A Division of Grolier Publishing
LONDON • NEW YORK • HONG KONG • SYDNEY
DANBURY, CONNECTICUT

CONTENTS

NORTH
AMERICA

PACIFIC
OCEAN

SOUT
AMERI

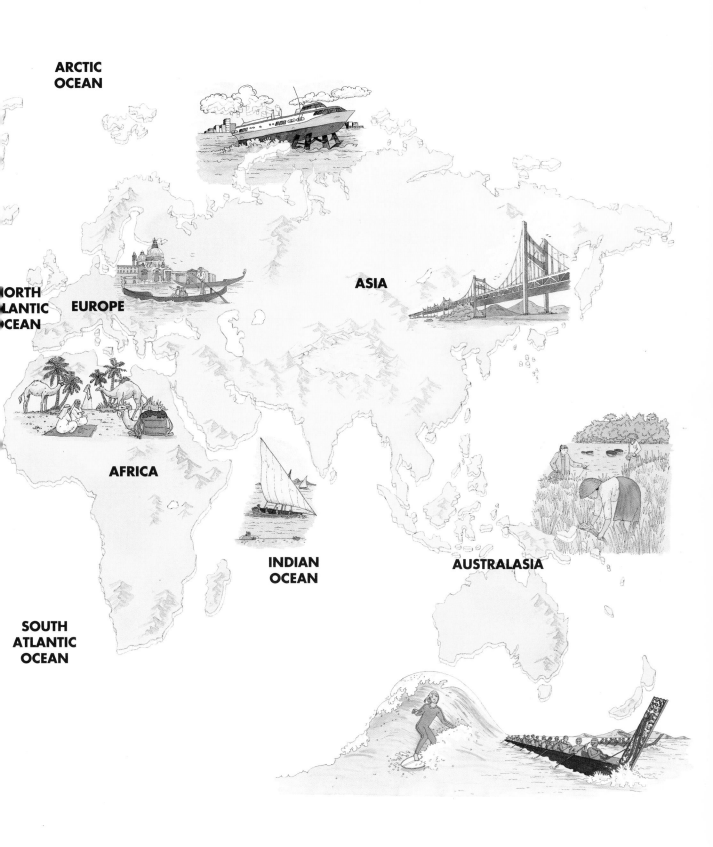

ARCTIC
OCEAN

NORTH
ATLANTIC
OCEAN

EUROPE

ASIA

AFRICA

INDIAN
OCEAN

AUSTRALASIA

SOUTH
ATLANTIC
OCEAN

INTRODUCTION

When seen from space, our planet looks blue. This is because more than seven-tenths of the Earth's surface is covered with water. Nearly all of it is in the salty oceans.

The largest and deepest ocean is the Pacific. It is bigger than all the land on Earth put together. The Atlantic is the second largest. The Indian Ocean is the third largest ocean. The smallest, the Arctic, is a shallow ocean surrounded by land to the far north of the globe. For much of the year, it is covered in ice.

Most of the fresh, unsalty water is locked in the frozen polar ice caps and mountain glaciers. The rest is in the rocks beneath our feet, in lakes, rivers, and ponds.

Many large cities evolved beside rivers because they provided water for drinking and also for growing crops. Rivers were also the best means of transporting goods. Today, the sea, lakes, and rivers are popular places for sailing and other watersports.

In this book, we look at water around the world – how people and animals use it, and how it affects and forms landscapes and environments. We do this by looking at maps of different areas of the world.

NORTH AMERICA

ATLAN
OCEA

**SOUT
AMERI**

The Nile delta
The wide, fan-shaped mouth of a river is called a delta. The satellite photograph on the right shows the huge delta of the Nile River in Africa. The Nile is the longest river in the world. It is 4,135 miles long.

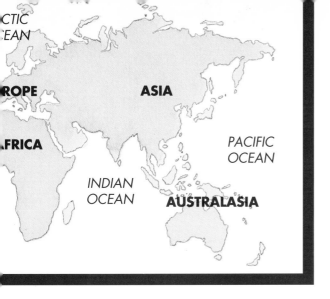

CTIC
CEAN

ROPE

ASIA

AFRICA

PACIFIC OCEAN

INDIAN OCEAN

AUSTRALASIA

- As a globe shows, the Earth is round. A map is a drawing of the Earth's surface on a flat piece of paper. On each page of this book an arrow shows which part of the globe is drawn flat on the map.

- A compass tells you which direction is north, south, east, and west. There is a compass like this one on each map.

N
W E
S

- At the bottom of each map there is a scale. The scale allows you to work out how far the real distance is between places on the map.

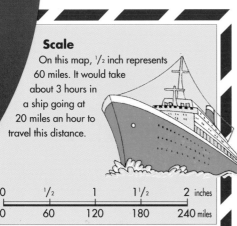

Scale
On this map, $1/2$ inch represents 60 miles. It would take about 3 hours in a ship going at 20 miles an hour to travel this distance.

| 0 | $1/2$ | 1 | $1 1/2$ | 2 inches |
| 0 | 60 | 120 | 180 | 240 miles |

Map symbols:

These picture symbols on the map show landmarks and activities in selected places in the world.

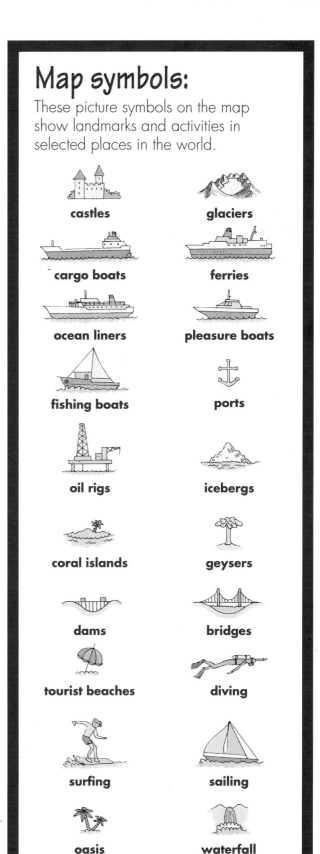

castles

glaciers

cargo boats

ferries

ocean liners

pleasure boats

fishing boats

ports

oil rigs

icebergs

coral islands

geysers

dams

bridges

tourist beaches

diving

surfing

sailing

oasis

waterfall

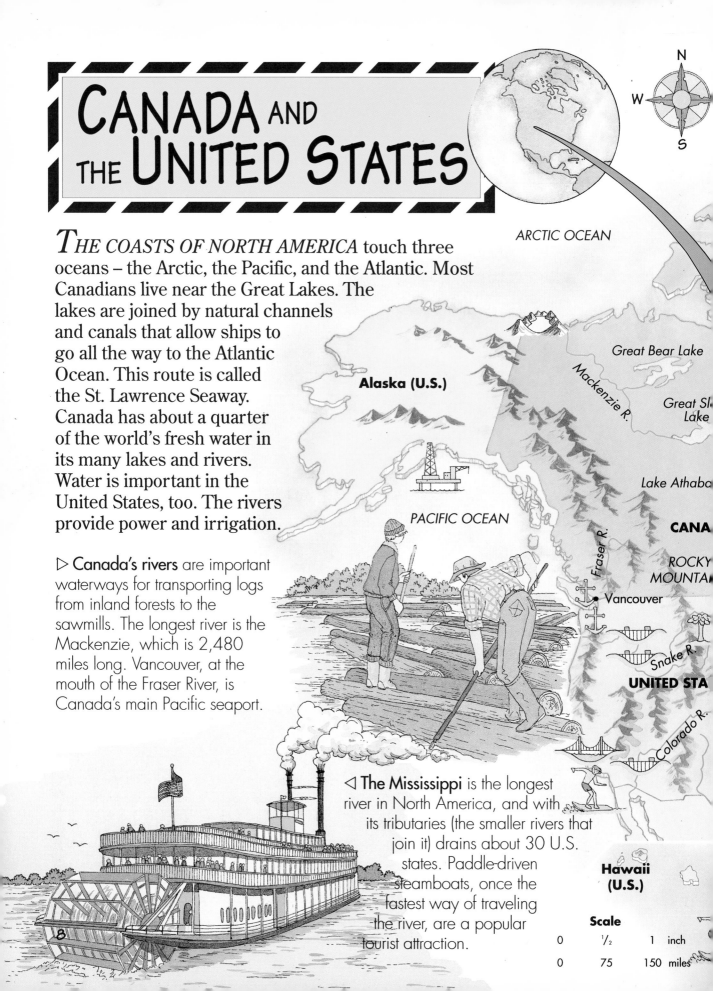

CANADA AND THE UNITED STATES

ARCTIC OCEAN

THE COASTS OF NORTH AMERICA touch three oceans – the Arctic, the Pacific, and the Atlantic. Most Canadians live near the Great Lakes. The lakes are joined by natural channels and canals that allow ships to go all the way to the Atlantic Ocean. This route is called the St. Lawrence Seaway. Canada has about a quarter of the world's fresh water in its many lakes and rivers. Water is important in the United States, too. The rivers provide power and irrigation.

▷ **Canada's rivers** are important waterways for transporting logs from inland forests to the sawmills. The longest river is the Mackenzie, which is 2,480 miles long. Vancouver, at the mouth of the Fraser River, is Canada's main Pacific seaport.

Great Bear Lake

Alaska (U.S.)

Mackenzie R.

Great Sl___ Lake

PACIFIC OCEAN

Lake Athaba___

CANA___

Fraser R.

ROCKY MOUNTA___

Vancouver

Snake R.

UNITED STA___

Colorado R.

◁ **The Mississippi** is the longest river in North America, and with its tributaries (the smaller rivers that join it) drains about 30 U.S. states. Paddle-driven steamboats, once the fastest way of traveling the river, are a popular tourist attraction.

Hawaii (U.S.)

Scale

0	½	1	inch
0	75	150	miles

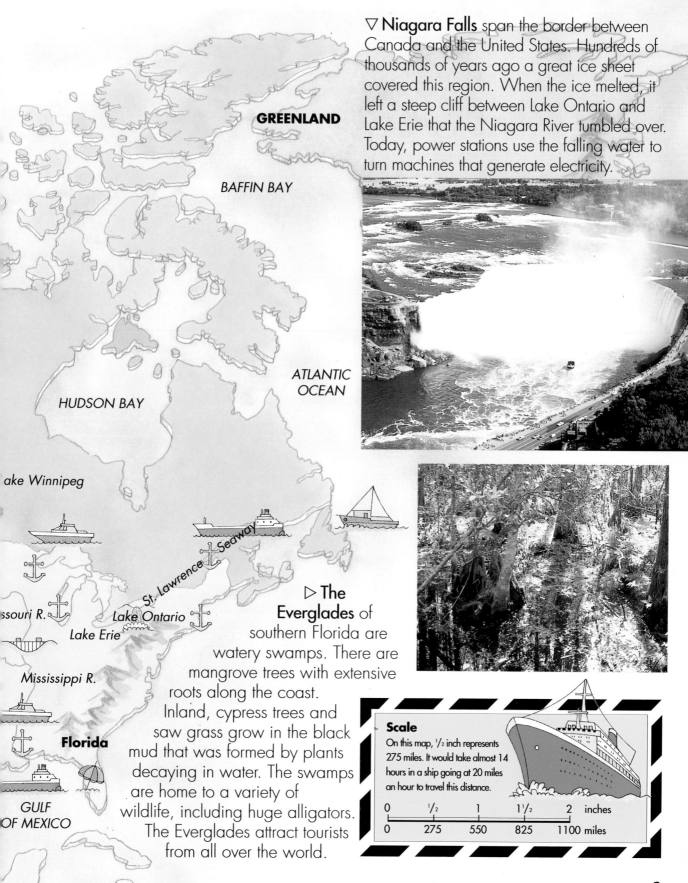

▽ **Niagara Falls** span the border between Canada and the United States. Hundreds of thousands of years ago a great ice sheet covered this region. When the ice melted, it left a steep cliff between Lake Ontario and Lake Erie that the Niagara River tumbled over. Today, power stations use the falling water to turn machines that generate electricity.

GREENLAND

BAFFIN BAY

ATLANTIC OCEAN

HUDSON BAY

ake Winnipeg

St. Lawrence Seaway

ssouri R.

Lake Ontario

Lake Erie

Mississippi R.

Florida

GULF OF MEXICO

▷ **The Everglades** of southern Florida are watery swamps. There are mangrove trees with extensive roots along the coast. Inland, cypress trees and saw grass grow in the black mud that was formed by plants decaying in water. The swamps are home to a variety of wildlife, including huge alligators. The Everglades attract tourists from all over the world.

Scale
On this map, ¹/₂ inch represents 275 miles. It would take almost 14 hours in a ship going at 20 miles an hour to travel this distance.

0	¹/₂	1	1¹/₂	2	inches
0	275	550	825	1100	miles

MEXICO, CENTRAL AMERICA,
AND THE CARIBBEAN ISLANDS

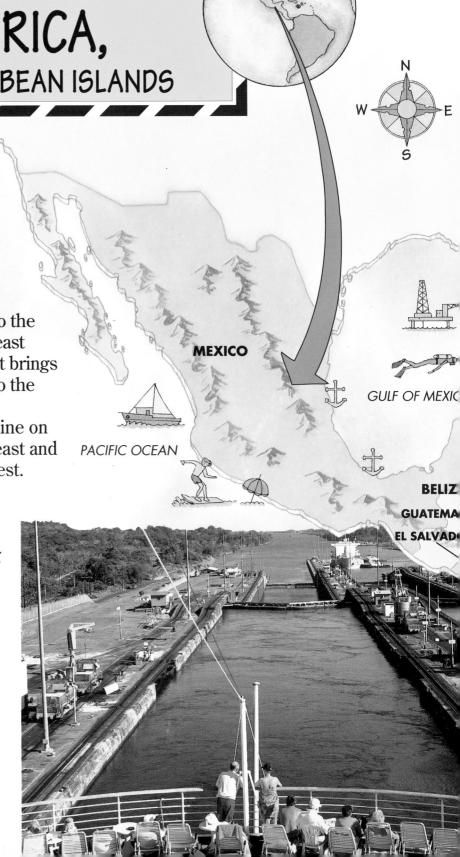

A WARM OCEAN CURRENT called the Gulf Stream starts in the Caribbean Sea. It flows right across the Atlantic Ocean and affects the climate of countries in Europe thousands of miles away. The current flows into the Gulf of Mexico and up the east coast of the United States. It brings a warm and moist climate to the coastal areas in its path.

Mexico has a long coastline on the Gulf of Mexico to the east and the Pacific Ocean to the west. Both bodies of water have merging cold and warm currents, which produce some of the richest fishing zones in the world.

N
W E
S

MEXICO

GULF OF MEXIC

PACIFIC OCEAN

BELIZ
GUATEMA
EL SALVAD

▷ **The Panama Canal** is a man-made shortcut between the Pacific and Atlantic oceans. It was opened in 1914 and is 50 miles long. A ship takes eight hours to make the journey and has to go through six locks.

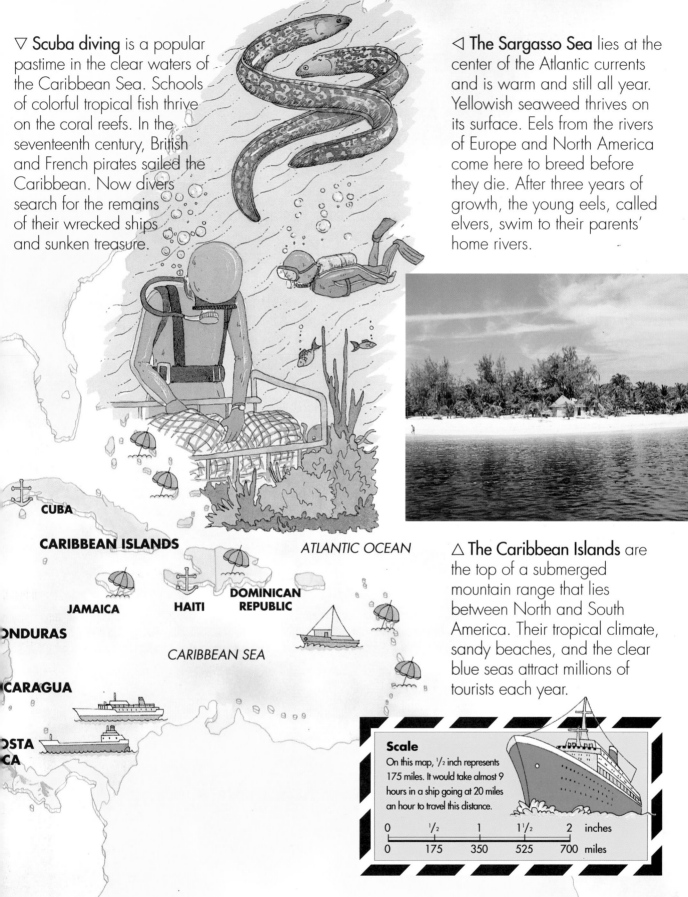

▽ **Scuba diving** is a popular pastime in the clear waters of the Caribbean Sea. Schools of colorful tropical fish thrive on the coral reefs. In the seventeenth century, British and French pirates sailed the Caribbean. Now divers search for the remains of their wrecked ships and sunken treasure.

◁ **The Sargasso Sea** lies at the center of the Atlantic currents and is warm and still all year. Yellowish seaweed thrives on its surface. Eels from the rivers of Europe and North America come here to breed before they die. After three years of growth, the young eels, called elvers, swim to their parents' home rivers.

△ **The Caribbean Islands** are the top of a submerged mountain range that lies between North and South America. Their tropical climate, sandy beaches, and the clear blue seas attract millions of tourists each year.

CUBA

CARIBBEAN ISLANDS

ATLANTIC OCEAN

JAMAICA

HAITI

DOMINICAN REPUBLIC

ONDURAS

CARIBBEAN SEA

CARAGUA

OSTA CA

Scale
On this map, 1/2 inch represents 175 miles. It would take almost 9 hours in a ship going at 20 miles an hour to travel this distance.

0	1/2	1	1 1/2	2	inches
0	175	350	525	700	miles

11

SOUTH AMERICA

SOUTH AMERICA is a continent of contrasts. The Amazon basin in Brazil is the wettest place in the world; the Atacama Desert in Chile is the driest – parts of it have not had rain for over four hundred years. The continent is surrounded by two oceans – the Atlantic to the east and the Pacific to the west. Most people live in the coastal regions or beside the Amazon. On the Atlantic coast are the great cities of Rio de Janeiro and Buenos Aires. The eastern seaports handle most of South America's trade.

Three vast river systems – the Orinoco, the Amazon and the Paraná-Paraguay – are a source of fish and a means of transport to the interior of the continent. Ocean-going ships can travel over 990 miles (1,600 km) inland along the Amazon from the coast.

△ **Lake Titicaca** is a busy and important waterway. Passengers and goods are carried across the lake by steamships. The lake is 12,500 feet above sea level. It is the highest navigable lake in the world. The Uru people who live around Lake Titicaca catch fish in the reed beds, and their boats and houses are made from reeds.

PAC
OCE

▷ **The Humboldt current** flows north from frozen Antarctica along the coasts of Chile and Peru. The cold water is rich in plankton, microscopic animals, and plants. Shoals of small fish called anchovies eat the plankton. Fishermen catch anchovies in circular nets. They are made into fish meal for animal food and fertilizer.

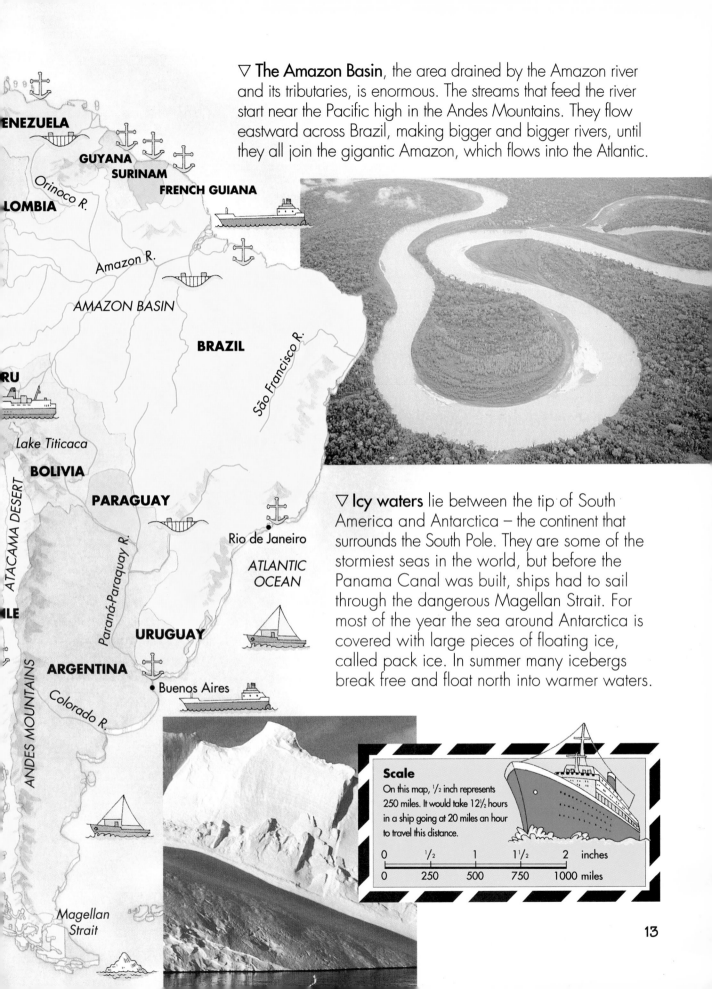

▽ **The Amazon Basin**, the area drained by the Amazon river and its tributaries, is enormous. The streams that feed the river start near the Pacific high in the Andes Mountains. They flow eastward across Brazil, making bigger and bigger rivers, until they all join the gigantic Amazon, which flows into the Atlantic.

▽ **Icy waters** lie between the tip of South America and Antarctica – the continent that surrounds the South Pole. They are some of the stormiest seas in the world, but before the Panama Canal was built, ships had to sail through the dangerous Magellan Strait. For most of the year the sea around Antarctica is covered with large pieces of floating ice, called pack ice. In summer many icebergs break free and float north into warmer waters.

Scale
On this map, 1/2 inch represents 250 miles. It would take 12 1/2 hours in a ship going at 20 miles an hour to travel this distance.

0	1/2	1	1 1/2	2	inches
0	250	500	750	1000	miles

Map labels: VENEZUELA, GUYANA, SURINAM, FRENCH GUIANA, COLOMBIA, Orinoco R., Amazon R., AMAZON BASIN, BRAZIL, São Francisco R., PERU, Lake Titicaca, BOLIVIA, PARAGUAY, Paraná-Paraguay R., Rio de Janeiro, ATLANTIC OCEAN, ATACAMA DESERT, CHILE, URUGUAY, ARGENTINA, Buenos Aires, Colorado R., ANDES MOUNTAINS, Magellan Strait

NORTHERN EUROPE

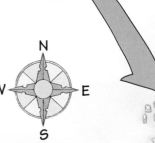

THE NORTH ATLANTIC OCEAN forms the western boundary of Europe. To the south lies the Mediterranean Sea. The northern boundary is formed by the icy Arctic Ocean. The North Atlantic contains some of the world's main fishing grounds.

The warm water of the Gulf Stream (see page 10) flows past the British Isles and northwest Europe. This makes the climate there much warmer than it would be otherwise. Abundant rainfall and many rivers make much of northern Europe green and fertile. Small lakes are common, too – Scotland is a country famed for its many fresh and seawater lakes, called lochs, and Finland has no less than 60,000 lakes!

ICELAND

ARCTIC OCEAN

N
W   E
S

SCOTLA

NORTHERN IRELAND

ATLANTIC OCEAN

IRELAND

WALES

ENGLAND

• Lor

Dover •

ENGLISH CHANNEL

BEL

BAY OF BISCAY

Loire R.

FRAN

Garonne R.

MEDITERRANE SEA

△ **Ferries** carry passengers and freight across the English Channel. Until 1994, all heavy traffic between England and mainland Europe went by sea. Now special trains carry passengers, cars, and trucks between Dover and Calais in the 31-mile-long Channel Tunnel in 35 minutes.

◁ **The fjords** of Norway were carved out by glaciers during the last ice age. This ended about 10,000 years ago, but at its height one third of the globe was covered with ice sheets extending as far south as St. Louis, Missouri, and London, England. Now the only permanent ice sheets are in Greenland and Antarctica.

◁ **Windmills** are used in The Netherlands to pump water from low-lying land. More than one third of the country lies below sea level. Engineers also build strong walls, called dykes, to keep the sea out.

▽ **Romantic castles** overlook the Rhine and the Danube as they wind through Europe. The Danube rises in the Black Forest and flows 1,776 miles across Europe to a swampy delta in the Black Sea. A canal links it to the Rhine, making an important waterway to the North Sea.

FINLAND

NORWAY

SWEDEN

BALTIC SEA

NORTH SEA

DENMARK

NETHERLANDS

Elbe R.

GERMANY

LUXEMBOURG

Vistula R.

POLAND

CZECH REPUBLIC

SLOVAKIA

Danube R.

AUSTRIA

SWITZERLAND

HUNGARY

ROMANIA

Scale
On this map, ¹/₂ inch represents 100 miles. It would take 5 hours in a ship going at 20 miles an hour to travel this distance.

0	¹/₂	1	1¹/₂	2	inches
0	100	200	300	400	miles

15

SOUTHERN EUROPE

*T*HE MEDITERRANEAN SEA is almost completely surrounded by land. Its only connection to the ocean is through the 10-mile-wide Strait of Gibraltar. Because it is almost landlocked, little new water can enter the Mediterranean. It is therefore very salty and almost tideless.

The climate in Southern Europe is warmer and drier than in Northern Europe. Numbers of tourists enjoy the warm sea and sandy beaches, but they are creating a growing problem. Popular beaches are polluted because sewage from the hotels is pumped directly into the sea, which has no currents to carry it away.

The Mediterranean Sea is in a region where there are earthquakes and volcanoes. Some of the many islands are extinct volcanoes.

▽ **The coast of southern Spain** is very popular for holidays. It is hot and dry during the summer, and like many other parts of the Mediterranean, there are beautiful beaches. People go to the Mediterranean to swim, sail, dive, water-ski, and windsurf. Many hotels have been built specially for tourists in the towns and cities around the Mediterranean coasts.

▷ **In salt pans,** seawater is channeled from one pool to the next. The heat from the sun evaporates the water and the salt becomes more concentrated until salt crystals form. These are raked up, dried, and packaged for use.

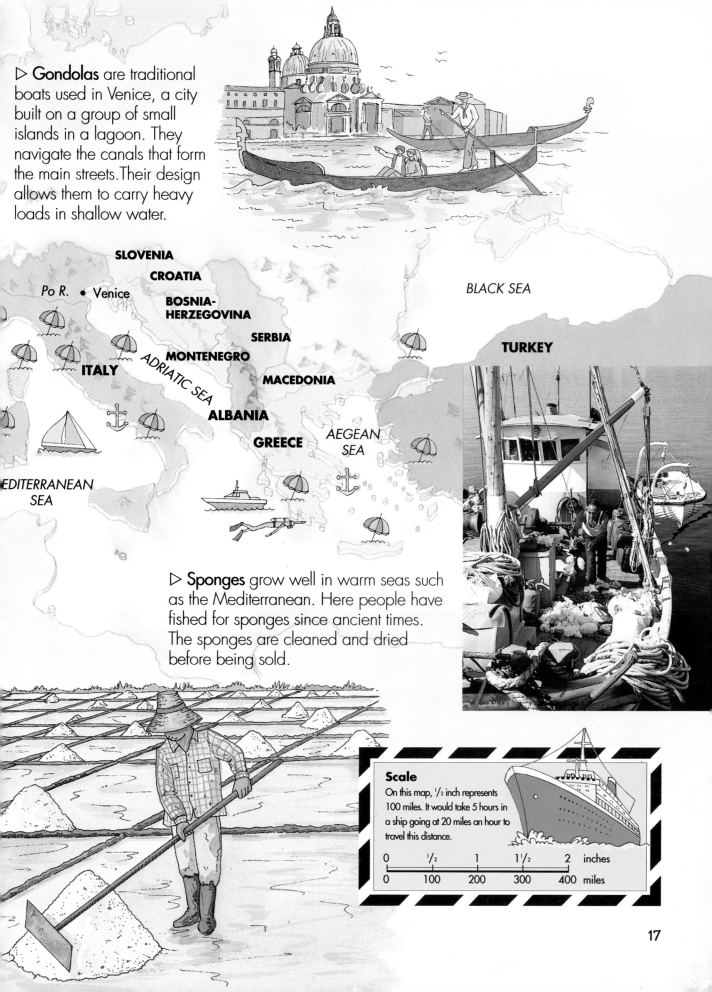

▷ **Gondolas** are traditional boats used in Venice, a city built on a group of small islands in a lagoon. They navigate the canals that form the main streets. Their design allows them to carry heavy loads in shallow water.

SLOVENIA
CROATIA
Po R. • Venice
BOSNIA-HERZEGOVINA
SERBIA
MONTENEGRO
ITALY
ADRIATIC SEA
MACEDONIA
ALBANIA
GREECE
AEGEAN SEA

BLACK SEA

TURKEY

EDITERRANEAN SEA

▷ **Sponges** grow well in warm seas such as the Mediterranean. Here people have fished for sponges since ancient times. The sponges are cleaned and dried before being sold.

Scale
On this map, ¹/₂ inch represents 100 miles. It would take 5 hours in a ship going at 20 miles an hour to travel this distance.

0	¹/₂	1	1¹/₂	2	inches
0	100	200	300	400	miles

AFRICA

In central Africa, around the equator, there are vast forests where the temperature is always high and it rains every day. These are the rainforests. They give way to tropical grasslands, which have a dry season and a wet season. In the north lies the Sahara, a desert that covers one third of Africa and is growing larger. Underneath the Sahara are vast supplies of water. Huge pipelines are being built to carry the water to coastal areas in the north. In the far north and far south of Africa, the climate is hot and dry in summer, and mild and wet in winter.

Africa is home to the world's longest river, the Nile. Lake Victoria is one of its sources. In the Rift Valley in East Africa, there is a chain of long, narrow, deep lakes where the continent is gradually being split apart.

MOROCCO

WESTERN SAHARA

ALGERIA

MAURITANIA

SAHARA DES

MALI

SENEGAL

THE GAMBIA

Niger R.

NIG

GUINEA BISSAU

GUINEA

SIERRA LEONE

IVORY COAST

BENIN

TOGO

LIBERIA

NIGER

GHANA

GUIN

ATLAN
OCEA

△ **An oasis** is a desert spring where water from deep under the ground bubbles to the surface. This water may flow from mountains hundreds of miles away. In a large oasis, palms give shade and farmers can grow vegetables.

◁ **The Victoria Falls** on the Zambezi River is 354 feet high and nearly 1¼ miles wide. The waterfall makes so much noise and spray that the local people call it "the smoke that thunders."

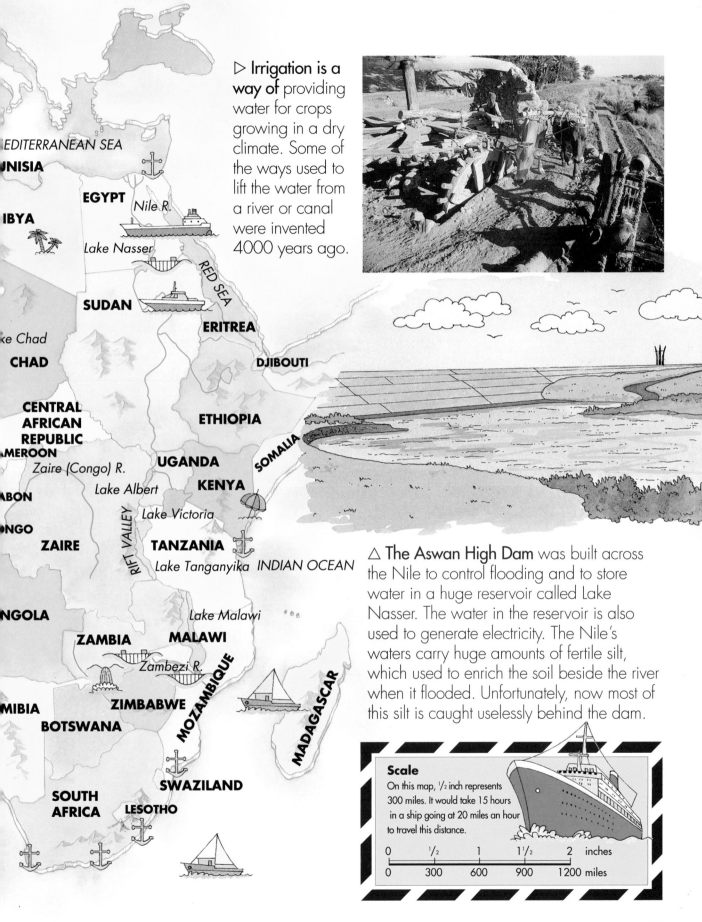

▷ **Irrigation is a way of** providing water for crops growing in a dry climate. Some of the ways used to lift the water from a river or canal were invented 4000 years ago.

MEDITERRANEAN SEA

TUNISIA

LIBYA

EGYPT

Nile R.

Lake Nasser

RED SEA

SUDAN

ERITREA

Lake Chad

CHAD

DJIBOUTI

CENTRAL AFRICAN REPUBLIC

CAMEROON

ETHIOPIA

Zaire (Congo) R.

UGANDA

SOMALIA

GABON

Lake Albert

KENYA

CONGO

Lake Victoria

RIFT VALLEY

ZAIRE

TANZANIA

Lake Tanganyika INDIAN OCEAN

ANGOLA

Lake Malawi

ZAMBIA

MALAWI

Zambezi R.

MOZAMBIQUE

NAMIBIA

ZIMBABWE

MADAGASCAR

BOTSWANA

SWAZILAND

SOUTH AFRICA

LESOTHO

△ **The Aswan High Dam** was built across the Nile to control flooding and to store water in a huge reservoir called Lake Nasser. The water in the reservoir is also used to generate electricity. The Nile's waters carry huge amounts of fertile silt, which used to enrich the soil beside the river when it flooded. Unfortunately, now most of this silt is caught uselessly behind the dam.

Scale
On this map, ¹/₂ inch represents 300 miles. It would take 15 hours in a ship going at 20 miles an hour to travel this distance.

0	¹/₂	1	1¹/₂	2	inches
0	300	600	900	1200	miles

RUSSIA
AND THE FORMER SOVIET STATES

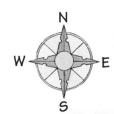

MUCH OF THE HUGE AREA occupied by Russia and the former Soviet States has a very cold climate. The northern coast borders the Arctic Ocean, which is a sea of ice. For several months of the year, rivers and lakes in the north and east are completely frozen. Lake Baikal is the world's deepest lake. It is 5,315 feet deep and contains a fifth of the world's fresh water.

Because of the severe climate in the north and east, the more densely populated areas are in the west. Here the land is well-drained and ideal for farming. The ports on the Baltic Sea are frozen during the winter. By contrast, in the south, the Black Sea is a popular tourist area with a warm, mild climate.

ARCTIC OCEAN

BARENTS SEA

BALTIC SEA

ESTONIA
LATVIA
LITHUANIA
BELARUS

Volga R.

Moscow

UKRAINE

MOLDOVA

Dnieper R.

Don R.

Volgograd

CASPIAN SEA

GEORGIA

BLACK SEA

AZERBAIJ

ARMENIA

◁ **The Volga** is Russia's most important waterway. Most of the river is navigable by hydrofoil, steamer, and cargo boats. Canals and rivers link the Volga to such major cities as Moscow and Volgograd, and to the Baltic.

▷ **Dams and reservoirs** help to regulate the flow of water of the Volga River so that it no longer floods. Water behind the dam is used to generate electric power and to irrigate the fields.

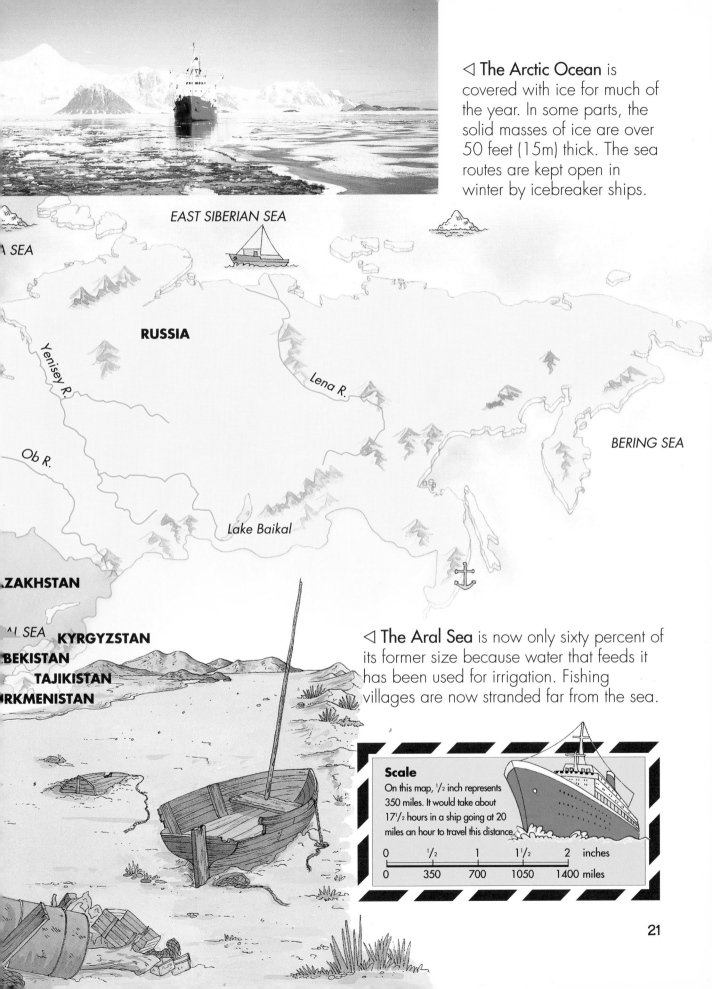

◁ **The Arctic Ocean** is covered with ice for much of the year. In some parts, the solid masses of ice are over 50 feet (15m) thick. The sea routes are kept open in winter by icebreaker ships.

EAST SIBERIAN SEA

A SEA

RUSSIA

Yenisey R.

Lena R.

Ob R.

BERING SEA

Lake Baikal

ZAKHSTAN

AL SEA **KYRGYZSTAN**

BEKISTAN

TAJIKISTAN

RKMENISTAN

◁ **The Aral Sea** is now only sixty percent of its former size because water that feeds it has been used for irrigation. Fishing villages are now stranded far from the sea.

Scale
On this map, ¹/₂ inch represents 350 miles. It would take about 17¹/₂ hours in a ship going at 20 miles an hour to travel this distance.

0	¹/₂	1	1¹/₂	2	inches
0	350	700	1050	1400	miles

THE MIDDLE EAST

MOST OF THE MIDDLE EAST has a hot climate and large areas are desert. The main rivers are the Tigris and Euphrates. It was here, about 7,000 years ago, that the first city civilization in the world grew up. The soils in the valley between them were made fertile by regular floods. To control the flooding, and to make sure that the floodwaters enriched the largest possible area, the people developed irrigation. The collection and distribution of water has remained a major concern for the people of the Middle East ever since.

The waters of the Persian Gulf are very shallow, with an average depth of only 84 feet. Its waters are warm, sometimes reaching 95°F in the summer. The Gulf is famous for its pearl-bearing oysters, but now its vast oil reserves are more important.

MEDITERRANEAN SEA

GAZA STRIP ISR.

Suez Canal Dead

Jordan

RED SEA

▷ **The dhow** is the traditional sailing boat of the Red Sea and the Gulf. Dhows were used by merchants who sailed in the Gulf thousands of years ago. They are still used for coastal trade and as fishing boats.

◁ **The Suez Canal** connects the Red Sea with the Mediterranean. It is one of the busiest shipping lanes in the world, but is too narrow for two large tankers to pass through at the same time. One of them has to wait in a turnout called a "loop."

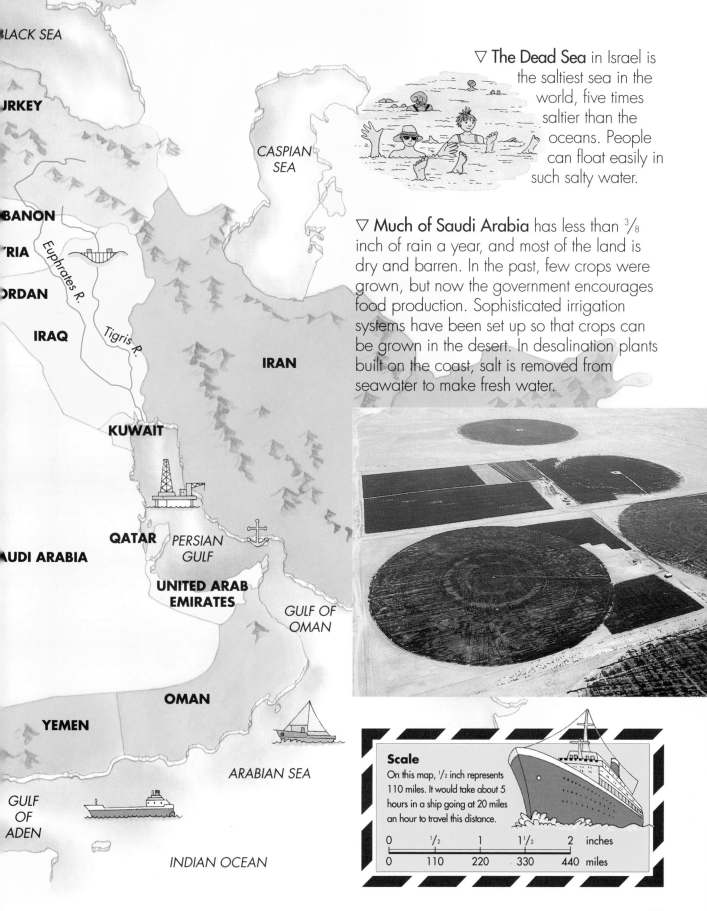

BLACK SEA

TURKEY

CASPIAN
SEA

LEBANON

SYRIA

JORDAN

IRAQ

Euphrates R.

Tigris R.

IRAN

KUWAIT

QATAR   PERSIAN
GULF

SAUDI ARABIA

UNITED ARAB
EMIRATES

GULF OF
OMAN

OMAN

YEMEN

ARABIAN SEA

GULF
OF
ADEN

INDIAN OCEAN

▽ **The Dead Sea** in Israel is the saltiest sea in the world, five times saltier than the oceans. People can float easily in such salty water.

▽ **Much of Saudi Arabia** has less than $\frac{3}{8}$ inch of rain a year, and most of the land is dry and barren. In the past, few crops were grown, but now the government encourages food production. Sophisticated irrigation systems have been set up so that crops can be grown in the desert. In desalination plants built on the coast, salt is removed from seawater to make fresh water.

Scale
On this map, $\frac{1}{2}$ inch represents 110 miles. It would take about 5 hours in a ship going at 20 miles an hour to travel this distance.

0	$\frac{1}{2}$	1	$1\frac{1}{2}$	2	inches
0	110	220	330	440	miles

23

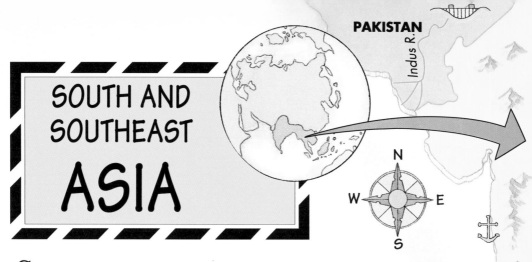

SOUTH AND SOUTHEAST ASIA

PAKISTAN

Indus R.

NEP

Varanasi

INDIA

N
W E
S

SRI LANKA

INDIAN OCEAN

S*NOW ON THE MOUNTAINS* between China and India melts and supplies water for four of the largest rivers in the world: the Irrawaddy, Indus, Ganges, and Brahmaputra. Where the rivers meet the sea, they drop mud and other material they carry to form deltas. People living on the Ganges-Brahmaputra delta in Bangladesh often lose their homes in heavy floods.

The Irrawaddy rises in the mountains near Myanmar's borders with China and India. At the beginning, it flows through rocky gorges and wooded hills. It grows wider as other rivers join it and then continues to the Bay of Bengal.

The monsoon winds that blow in this region bring heavy rain between April and September. In South Asia in particular, the rest of the year is dry.

▷ **Mangrove** trees grow in the muddy, tropical swamps of Indonesia. The extensive root system traps mud and silt. Mangrove seeds start to grow while still attached to the parent tree.

◁ **Coral islands** are found in warm, shallow tropical seas such as the Indian Ocean. The coral reefs that surround them are formed from the hard outer skeletons of tiny animals called coral polyps.

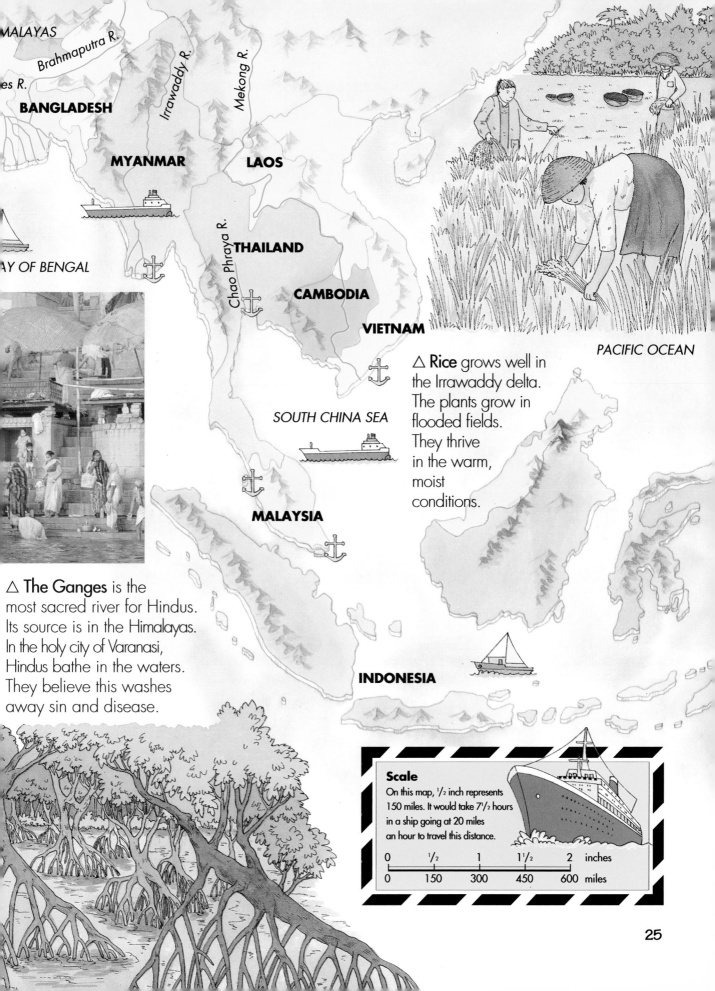

MALAYAS

Brahmaputra R.

es R.

BANGLADESH

Irrawaddy R.

Mekong R.

MYANMAR

LAOS

AY OF BENGAL

Chao Phraya R.

THAILAND

CAMBODIA

VIETNAM

SOUTH CHINA SEA

PACIFIC OCEAN

△ **Rice** grows well in the Irrawaddy delta. The plants grow in flooded fields. They thrive in the warm, moist conditions.

MALAYSIA

△ **The Ganges** is the most sacred river for Hindus. Its source is in the Himalayas. In the holy city of Varanasi, Hindus bathe in the waters. They believe this washes away sin and disease.

INDONESIA

Scale
On this map, ¹/₂ inch represents 150 miles. It would take 7¹/₂ hours in a ship going at 20 miles an hour to travel this distance.

0	¹/₂	1	1¹/₂	2	inches
0	150	300	450	600	miles

CHINA, JAPAN, AND THE PACIFIC ISLANDS

MORE THAN HALF of the world's population lives around the shores of the Pacific. In China, most people live around the river valleys of the southeast, where the first cities grew up. Here the Huang He and the Chang Jiang have provided water for crops and a means of transporting goods and people for more than 5,000 years. Rice is a staple food in China and Japan.

In Japan, most people live around the coast because the land is mountainous and forested. The Japanese are a great fishing people. Their fishing fleet is the largest in the world. The Philippines consists of over 7,000 islands. The islanders fish and grow rice.

Huang He R.

CHIN

Tibet

Chang Jiang R.

△ **The Huang He** gets its name, which means "yellow river," from its color. This shallow, slow-moving river begins in the Tibetan mountains and carries a precious cargo of yellow mud, which fertilizes the dry plains of northern China.

26

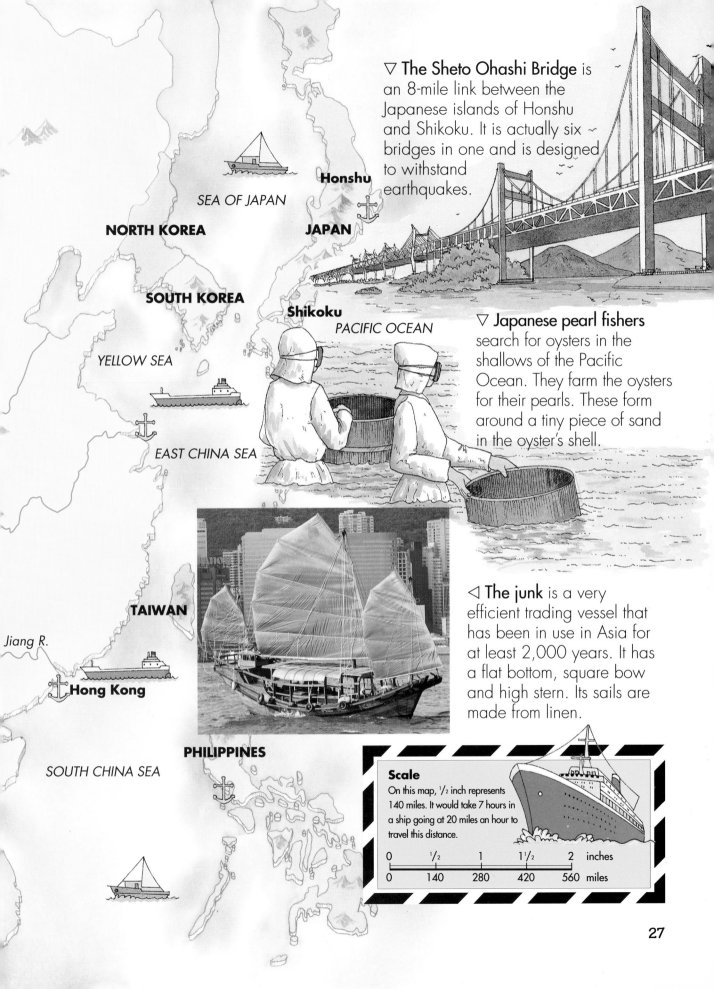

▽ **The Sheto Ohashi Bridge** is an 8-mile link between the Japanese islands of Honshu and Shikoku. It is actually six bridges in one and is designed to withstand earthquakes.

▽ **Japanese pearl fishers** search for oysters in the shallows of the Pacific Ocean. They farm the oysters for their pearls. These form around a tiny piece of sand in the oyster's shell.

◁ **The junk** is a very efficient trading vessel that has been in use in Asia for at least 2,000 years. It has a flat bottom, square bow and high stern. Its sails are made from linen.

Scale
On this map, 1/2 inch represents 140 miles. It would take 7 hours in a ship going at 20 miles an hour to travel this distance.

0	1/2	1	1 1/2	2	inches
0	140	280	420	560	miles

SEA OF JAPAN

Honshu

NORTH KOREA

JAPAN

SOUTH KOREA

Shikoku

PACIFIC OCEAN

YELLOW SEA

EAST CHINA SEA

TAIWAN

Jiang R.

Hong Kong

PHILIPPINES

SOUTH CHINA SEA

AUSTRALASIA

AUSTRALIA HAS THE LEAST rainfall of any continent. From the completely treeless Nullabor Plain in western Australia, to the tropical rainforests along its northern coasts, it is land of extremes. In the arid desert interior, called the outback, there are vast, mainly dry, salt lakes, such as Lake Eyre. These "lakes" sometimes fill up after rare storms. As rivers dry up during droughts, pools of water called "billabongs" are left. Dams across the Murray and Darling rivers store water for hydroelectric power stations.

New Zealand's warm, moist climate makes it ideal farming country. The southwest coast of South Island is called Fiordland because, like Norway, it has many narrow inlets. Auckland, the main port, has two harbors, one in the Pacific, the other in the Tasman Sea. To the south the cold seas around Antarctica are rich with plankton. The krill that eat plankton are food for fish, seals, and whales.

INDIAN OCEAN

AUSTRALIA

Lake Ey

NULLABOR PLAIN

Murr

▷ **Surfers** ride the crests of large waves off Bondi beach in Sydney, Australia. The sport was invented in this part of the world hundreds of years ago. The world's best surfing beaches are on coasts facing great expanses of ocean.

PACIFIC OCEAN

PUA NEW GUINEA

AT BARRIER REEF

CORAL SEA

eensland

ing R.

Sydney

TASMAN SEA

Auckland
Rotorua

NEW ZEALAND

◁ **The Great Barrier Reef,** off the coast of Queensland, Australia, is 1,260 miles long, the largest coral reef in the world. It started to grow about 18 million years ago and covers an area twice as big as Iceland. The reef is now a marine park, with zones for sports activities and tourism. However it is threatened by pollution, mining, and rising sea levels.

▷ **Rotorua** is famous for its thermal springs. In the volcanic North Island of New Zealand, heat from deep inside the Earth turns water into steam. This geothermal energy is used to generate electricity.

▽ **The Maori war canoe** is now used only for ceremony. The Maoris were the first inhabitants of New Zealand. Their war canoes were decorated with carved wood.

Scale
On this map, ¹/₂ inch represents 250 miles. It would take about 12¹/₂ hours in a ship going at 20 miles an hour to travel this distance.

0	¹/₂	1	1¹/₂	2 inches
0	250	500	750	1000 miles

THE WATER WORKS

WATER IS NEVER STILL for long. Above the earth it moves about in the clouds. In the oceans it moves in currents of warm and cold water, and in the tides. On land it flows down hill to the sea. High in the mountains small streams join together to form a river. At first, the river flows through high-sided valleys, over waterfalls, and through rapids. As the river reaches flat land, it slows down and develops broad bends called meanders before reaching the sea.

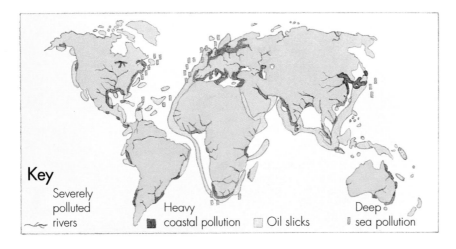

Key

Severely polluted rivers

Heavy coastal pollution

Oil slicks

Deep sea pollution

△ **Waste** from cities and factories pollutes more and more of the water in our rivers. All plants and animals depend on water for life. We need water to grow crops and to use in factories and homes – above all, we need clean water to drink.

▷ **Ocean currents** move in circular patterns as they are swept along by the wind. They turn clockwise in the Northern Hemisphere and counterclockwise in the Southern Hemisphere. Some are warm; others are cold. Ocean currents change the climate and the weather.

Key

Warm currents

Cold currents

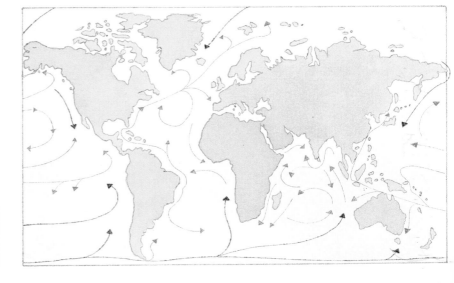

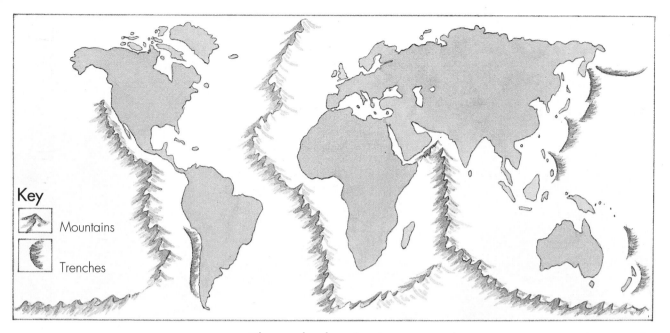

Key
Mountains
Trenches

△ **The seabed** under the oceans has mountains, trenches, and cliffs far higher, deeper, and larger than any found on land. Lava wells up from active volcanoes, cools, and then hardens to form a new ocean crust. The pressure caused by volcanic action forces whole continents to drift apart very slowly.

▽ **In the water cycle** the sun heats the water in rivers, lakes, and oceans and turns some of it into vapor in the air. The air then rises and cools, forms clouds, and it rains again. The total amount of water on earth remains the same in a never-ending journey called the water cycle.

△ **Tides** rise and fall two times each day. These are caused mainly by the moon. When the moon is directly over an ocean, its gravity pulls the water, making it bulge. The spin of the earth causes water to bulge on the opposite side of the earth, too. There are two high tides and two low tides every 24 hours.

Index